MW01179049

To unrequited love.

Let's split us in half

So that the falcon spends his days protecting

the mourning dove

Let's cut us in two

So that the shad understands that although the

Eagle has the power to eat it,

It chooses not to eat her

Come on love,

Let's divide us into halves

Because you tell me "let me realize how

powerful you are"

& so that the rabbit will look up at the hawk in

reverence

Let's split us into two

God,

Let me know the smell of roses without

touching their thorns

Let me fall into arms & not to feet

Please don't let me die without having known

happiness,

She prayed

& then God created man

For man she lit her way into darkness

Becoming his fire in frost

All without betraying her pain to anyone

Until, having realized that she'd silently fallen

onto rose thorns,

She looked to God

& God told her

"Above love is freedom"

I was there

Where all of the mirrors were waiting for your reflection

I was there

Where all of the rivers were waiting for your introspection

I was there

Through all of your guises

You are many years late, but I am still glad to see you

I was there

Waiting to tell you that "if God forgives us so knocked down, who are we to say no to each other?"

For you, I can give everything that I have

If only I know that my loving you is not in vain

For you, I can give everything that I will be

If only I know that you have the strength to go

to the end

For you I'd consider happiness giving you the

whole world every hour

If only I know that you will not betray me on

the road

But the point is still not this

The main thing is that my love is not an empty

phrase,

Not an invention

But what I see in you

The hope of being whole & not fragmented

Everyday my soul asks me

"Where is he?"

"Why aren't you with him?"

Then l remind it again of your rejection

& it responds with

"Again?"

"Still?"

& l answer

"Yes. Still"

Her name is enough to traumatize my soul

To make it tremble

The woman who uncovered the secret

She is the yardstick by which I now measure

my self-worth

My womanhood

The woman who discovered the keys to the

secret

She is my antithesis in one breath

My idol in the next

The woman that I think about almost as much

as I think about you

From me she stole the unthinkable

The woman who won your love

How difficult it is to describe a love in which

between the first & second breath,

there is always disappointment

How foolish it is to know such a love but to not

answer its doubts

Either in oneself or others

How desperate one must be to play dice using

their heart's flesh

Continuously cutting it on the glass of

someone long ago broken inside

How naive one must be to believe in their

uniqueness in the face of a love which will not

stoop to drink of them

May our love's silence sing those words which
we ourselves fear uttering

May our souls' connection continue to never
tolerate labels on itself

& with bated breath, may we continue being
the object of each other's hopes

But, if God forbid, in ourselves too we reach
the limit of our love which we meet in others,

May we nevertheless continue to be the
yardstick by which we measure the capacity of
human love

Because even dead, you are much better than
all the living

I found myself another rose

But his thorns don't prick me

So to keep myself alive

I replay our parting, sharper than needles, in
my mind

Because just like your love, it didn't leave me
indifferent

In a love where sparks fly only from quarrels,

I stay because I feel that it would be unworthy to give up

But rarely do you not wipe your feet on my soul

& as children fail to be disappointed by a bad parent

So I too am never disappointed by you

Because of the timid promises which lead me on

But little did we know of the quiet hatred which you awakened within me

& even now,

Little do you know of the emptiness of my words when you tell me that you love me

Little do you know that as firewood turns into ash in fire,

So my answer burns out in the flames of my resentment

Somewhere in this world lives a fallen woman with the face of purity

Who swears that there's a real man out there who exists just for her

Somewhere in this world is a weak woman carrying a cross

Pouring all of her worship on the scales of such a real man

Swearing that he exists because she exists

Somewhere in this world lives a woman

Who swears that this real man is the gap between who she is & who she wants to be

Somewhere in this world is a woman who has all of the imaginary promises of such a real man imprinted on her skin

Somewhere in this world

I wish that they'd told me about a sky with torn
edges
& that learning as a lover is like engraving in
stone,
That the sunrises would be dark in me once
you disappear
& that I'd spend your absence fantasizing
about other men,
Who, in reality, would be you disguised in
various faces
That it happens that humility is the only way
out
But that getting there could kill everything
alive inside

May you drink to others, but I have left

For I no longer await you on my shore,

Expecting you to return with apologies & the

healing of my old wounds

May you drink to others, but I have left

For I have built happiness on the ruins of my

heart's shreds

Not allowing it to be the case that you have

ruined life for me

May you drink to others, but I have left

For I am enjoying being myself

A self free of wonders about where your heart

lies, or with whom

May you drink to others, but I have left

For I am now at peace with our past

& without fear, without loss

When I met you, I'd hoped that your eyes would penetrate my very soul, & see me real, without a mask
I'd hoped that you wouldn't need words to understand how lonely & painful it has been for me to live on this earth
When I met you, I'd hoped that your eyes would penetrate my very soul, & see me real, with the scars that saddle my soul
I'd hoped that you would sense the inexplicable burden that I carry in my chest
When I met you, I'd hoped that your eyes would penetrate my very soul, & see me real, & just know of the invisible tears that I shed in the silence of empty rooms
I'd hoped that your heart would hurt with my pain
When I met you, I'd hoped that your eyes would penetrate my very soul, & see me real, ugly & weak but not be disappointed in me
I'd hoped that you'd be able to see the kind of wild power that lives in my sad eyes
When I met you, I'd hoped that God would grant me the opportunity to see, in your eyes, a reflection of a holistic embodiment of myself
I'd hoped that you'd be a person in whom I could take time out from fate
But the mind will anticipate the answer & turn away if it does not want to hear it
As yours must've anticipated my hopes

Before I was born,

I was shown my whole life,

& all I remember from it was talk of a mirror

brother,

To whom I would have a natural affinity,

& with whom I am in different lives but in the

same frequencies

Now, ever since having met you,

I can't help the feeling of the most powerful

déjà vue,

Or the inkling of a synergistic effect,

& I just want you to know that all of a sudden,

In my hopeless arms,

I hold a big heart for you

It's like the elephant in the room

The splinter in my heart

The heartache which glares me right in the face

But that I am too frightened & ashamed to address

It's like a festering wound

The constant ache that I've succumbed to

That I've accepted as part of myself

Because I don't know how to rid myself of it

They're like ...

The tears that should be falling but aren't

Because I have them for expressing you not loving me,

But I have no form of expressing the pain of you choosing her over me l met one artist, & he taught me a love for which there is still no language

A love who's words dictionaries have not yet been created that would translate

A love in which one word is sometimes a whole story,

A whole passion with all its shades

& lovers' sincerity is a separate form of art

l met an artist, & he showed me a love that can only be seen from the point of view of eternity

A love which teaches you to forgive unspoken words

A love in which the wounds that lovers awaken with every morning are filled with love again for their partners,

Twisting their soul in warmth

& something reassuring instead is left in the form of happiness

l met one artist, & he taught me a love in which what's inside is always burning

I want absolute silence in my head,

So as not to hear my voice reproaching me for
all of the former mistakes I've made in
protecting myself

Because I failed to realize that history is long
& that on our way to each other, we would see
different people

Not by coincidence, but because there are no
unnecessary meetings

Thus I broke after having witnessed you with
her

Out of fear that you had lost the plot & gone
astray

But I pray that God have mercy & for me, have
you leave the door open

Since after all, human relations are like crystal,
not iron

& even he has a scar left with love

If you have lost a loved one in my face,

It is because you have left me with an empty

heart in hand,

& with disappointment stuck in my throat,

For which you will not be forgiven

Remember this when you start bargaining with

me for what you need

The due will come

& all the best always has a deadline

I used to think that my eyes need to be blue to reflect a sky full of stars
& my teeth, seamless, in order for you to carry the light of my smile through the years
That my hair needs to be straight in order to redo myself,
& that my skin needs to be lighter for you to choose me like there is no one else in the room,
That I need to speak your language in order for you to live respecting your choice in me,
& that I need to be more gentle
In essence, I used to wish that I was her
But these days, I only wish you the best with her

Thank you for your support in purchasing this book. Please further support by sharing it with your loved ones. If you have an Instagram account, follow this book's page @muchbetterthanalltheliving & tag it in your posts in order to be featured.

CPSIA information can be obtained
at www.ICGtesting.com
Printed in the USA
LVHW071638031120
670613LV00010B/414

9 781715 655198